Bittersweet Gallerias is the reminiscence of the past, present and of what I hope to be the future of my life, in what I call mini premonitions (in no particular order).

I open my heart in the form of sharing my semisweet memories with you all.

Supposedly you may connect with my pain or my joys, nevertheless…

Let's sail on the unpredicted skies together.

I'd rather suffocate on noxious skies, than see you walk

away from me, than to hear you be happy with another,

than to prepare a lifetime without you.

So go ahead shroud me and conjure away your story.

We know the veracity of your truths.

Do I deserve the unworldly things?

Am I supposed to accept all hurt and yet still provide forgiveness?
To selfishness?
Why?
Is my heart not pure?
Does one attract dark matter?
People become so accustomed to all things superfluous
That input becomes uncredited furthermore unappreciated.

As much as one desires to treasure another in life the shear fact of observing and adoring each breath or movement made remains disheartened worship my call as my soul attracts yours

If to die was to live,
I'd spend an eternity dying a million ways just to spend extra time with you.

If to cry was for joy,
Id shed it all for a grand portion more happiness together.

If organs could split,
To you, my heart I would give and bleed 'til I am dry.

If pain was pleasurable,
I'd withstand as much ache as I could for you.

But we live to die, so our time is limited.
We cry because we become wounded,
Organs do not split although a part of me has latched on to you and submerged within your tegument,
And the pain, that would eliminate my ability to love you so profoundly.

This intense feeling of sick I feel inside is all due to this being that shows no sentiment in the world.

Is this exaggeration?

Not even in the slightest!

Can I hate such a spiritual person?
My mind, body and soul would not let me

There is no fault, no imperfections, and no wrong that I can see. This is not love, nor is it lust, but it surely is more than such...
Of the desire!

This is not infatuation, for infatuation is merely temporarily and simple minded.
But this is long overdue and for the Lord above to bless my eyes as well as this earth to see and be in the same presence as such a fine creation.
I'm grateful.

But for as long as this human is not fully mine to care for the sickness shall remain.

Clocked amongst a sensation in which even I cannot begin to fathom.

A glance drives one to become sentimental.

Eloquently expressed words are admired.

Yet, it is the utter sense one craves even throughout my dreams...

The intangible presence, the warmth upon my neck, as well as the ear, of such depth in a voice, sustains one to be persistently mesmerised.

(Mon ode to you)

One couldn't express this openly to you.

What started off as friends, turned into lust, formed into something a bit more, like suddenly this man, baby, I will always adore.

I can't comprehend how such a fine specimen, can be so amazing and like poison at the same damn time.
Oh my,

I've never been so discombobulated and able to show my emotions at the same damn time.
For the reason that once one falls in love, one ends up falling for something one wishes one did not acknowledge once before.

The realisation that I was amidst the atmosphere and close to cloud nine could majorly descend, simply due to misconception not that my feelings are mixed, they've never been so clear for a beautiful creature.
But for the fact of the matter he may dismiss them…

The very idea of him fills one with excitement, makes
one scared, shy, protected, proud and passionate.
All these once buried under... turned me heartless
because I did not want to feel them alone.

Yet they arise time and time again.

Retained, restricted, motionless...

Silence, excruciating,

Forceful,

Confined, inanimate, suffocating, dyspnoeic,

Revolting, degraded, violated, impure.

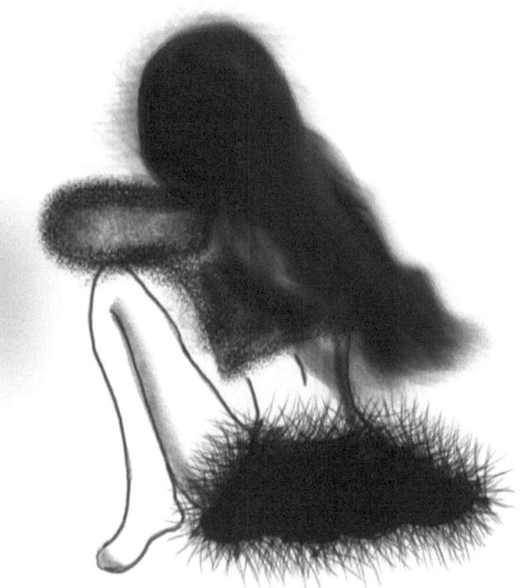

You etched your tempestuous pursuit of pleasure,
looped within my occipital lobe in anguish.

A mystery,

Overshadowed by the form of a black sky.
Should I proceed to see what I might expose or should I turn a blind eye and wait to see if it will pursue me?

This... enigma is it emotion, that seems to struggle to find its way to speak?

Is it the battle of the state of mind and the heart?

The mentally and the physically?

Either way it's reducing my supply of air, slowly, surely this is a moment that's surreal, but somehow I want to seize and cherish it.

Could this be the figment of my imagination, of my dreams?

Possibly.

Blinded by the fog before me, I'm met with a grasp in my hand and a masculine, overwhelming, but alluring whisper to my ear with such a sweet seductive scent as I recall.

Protected is the feeling I perceive by this being, weakened, not by force, but by the beauty of his heart.

Should I progress the situation to see what sequence is to become or should I position myself away... and wait for this journey to commence?

Torn between the choices as the repercussions of my actions may not be what I had hoped!

But if my existence was to mean anything in this universe at that secluded memorable time then the heart will speak throughout the tongue.

Here take these hands,
For only they, can feel yours.
Let ones lips gently grace yours, as these lips are meant, for only yours.

Here embrace ones words to continue to build and strengthen you.

Feel ones love, through each journey made, whilst feeling fingertips through your hair. Through each spiritual and emotional connection.
To capture your essence, once again, my best friend, my highs, my lows, my best, my life, I am yours, my heart is yours, I will love you as my friend until our hearts reunite once again my dove.

Formalities and certain obligations, define those whom live amongst the dead, those whom have not yet lived, have not raged, have not felt love, lust, sadness, deep darkness that no other feels or can ever perceive, an intoxicating high that is so surreal yet can be disastrous once it plummets down to reality, the struggle to breathe has never been clearer!

The loneliness has never been so strong. The mere fact that no-one has the slightest idea of how ones twisted outtake compared to the ordinary is...

However, our individual perceptions on life are the way we are made. Lost in my own emotions is how I am.

What I once worshipped,

your every word,

which was almost as sanctifying as you were...

*Is now all but dust, the ashes of your cremated bullsh*t.*

Our 'firsts' were always memorable.

I never thought that would include a first without you.

When negativity constantly flows into your direction... and you try your upmost best to be as much positive as you can... because deep inside you are in a vividly darkest haze... suffocating... trying to swim to the beautiful colours above... which become increasingly difficult to reach... as your energy shifts elsewhere.
Why?!
Why me?!
I find myself questioning this a lot lately.
With no one to answer my question, or questions. I feel lost more and more each day. Insecure and anxious, I've become to realise that even at your worst, there isn't a soul to turn to, but within yourself when you close yourself from the world so much so that you shut everyone out.

Have a drink?
Fall asleep?
Stay confined?
Maybe tomorrow, I'll go.
I want to escape
From here?
From myself?
I can't breathe
There's still so much to see,
So much to do,
To love,
To love...

I've been on my own for quite a while,
So cold,
I've forgotten how to... Love,
To fall in the same velocity and speed.
Oh, how I have fallen in love and wrapped my arms of the idea of you already.
Will you catch me?...

I need someone other than myself to confide in.
Someone to share our dreams with.
Fast forward to our laughs, fights and home.
Our wedding will be spectacular and the babies, the babies will dance like us.
Too premature?

•*Sometimes my thoughts run a mock of me, I wonder sometimes whether I am in a loop - Anxious*

Do not stop the sweet records that you play,
For they are majestic innocent lullabies.

The sweet sensation that is your voice is as though I am in a psychedelic universe graciously swimming through the ripples of a harmonic oceanic air cavity.

I thought my mind could tolerate the burns,
That my heart could heal the scars,
To some extent, I imagined I would become immune to the emotions, I thought had dissolved.

Suppressed, revived, alive, yet somewhat hidden,
Liberate me, divulge, disguise no longer.
Bedazzle me, capture me,
Simplify the hurt,
Specs of atoms, in hiatus until it issues a catastrophe.
Graze upon my...
Create an aura... blindly
Breathe gently around my...
Sensually Caress...
Amorously...

...

Impressive to attract a mind in such a way.

I wish that I could stop this pain, stop this abundance of love that I have for you.

That I could not feel the admiration and adoration that you once had for me, pass on to another.

That I could not witness another standing with what is, and will always, be my truest, purest, love......

I wish that I could stop the dreams I have for you, yet again, it is the only chance I have to feel your embrace, see you laugh or entwine our hands once more.

My heart will continue to weep for you.

These eyes... sheds for you...

These lips desire to say honeyed words.

When she walked in the room you knew...

How breathtakingly ravishing she was, despite how precarious she was, such a shame you failed to notice the strings she pulled thinking you could knead her.

You had a taste of her poison and suffered from her licentious activities. What was my all was another lifeless body to her.

Imagine sailing the seas
Against the bitter tides
Only for you to overthrow me.

I mourned so many nights,
Of my loss of you.
I wonder exactly, did you for me?

Such a heavenly face,
As the rays graciously chooses how to portray a prince who will become my king,
whom has encapsulated my heart from the strenuous maze...
into the succeeding treasury.

Let's embed ourselves amongst the stars, a place of serenity for just you and me.

When I am apart from him, I am perpetually exasperated with

him,

But when I see him, my goodness,

When I see that beautifully crafted face, that smiles at me with

so much love and admiration.

I am unbelievably serene

Let's run away you and I,
Let's become drunk of the significant highs that is our sentimental element continuously rising.

Let us engage in the thundering requisitions of one another.
Pierced and pouring...
Now or not at all!!!

I am broken, yes
I am my worst critic, yes!!!
Many minds fight to appear through...
Do not be fooled...
I am graceful,
I flourish, not in appearance, blooming from within.
I am too much of myself, excuse that, I am constantly evolving, cope with that

I do not run...
I do what you cannot.
I glide like a dove, to where I desire.
I flow with the skies and shine blindly.
I am the eruption causing the volcanic fires to glaze down the mountains.

Do not deceive yourself and think that you are my puppet master.

Majority of the people today become accustomed to irrelevant negative issues either to their own lives or towards that of which we breathe, feel, yet subconsciously admire on a daily basis, however, if that, of which was cherished is about to diminish ... and all we had were a mere final five seconds... to capture the essence of that, in which was provided yet greatly undervalued...

How that time would be spent, simply depends on the individual in question.

All I can see is darkness,
That is until you are near,
Then appear the stars

The room that was filled, has slowed down significantly... and all that is felt, an abundance of excitement.

Heart flutters and the sound of the world diminishes...
the reason...
you...
like an opiate.

He still has that love in his eyes, from when we first met
And I too the feeling merging beneath my flesh, deep in the layers of my platelets.

We can frame our impending outlook with our snapshots of the past.
Compose something magnetically sensational, the two of us.

For a time, yes you were pretty to look at...

I never thought that my body would be your template of torture.

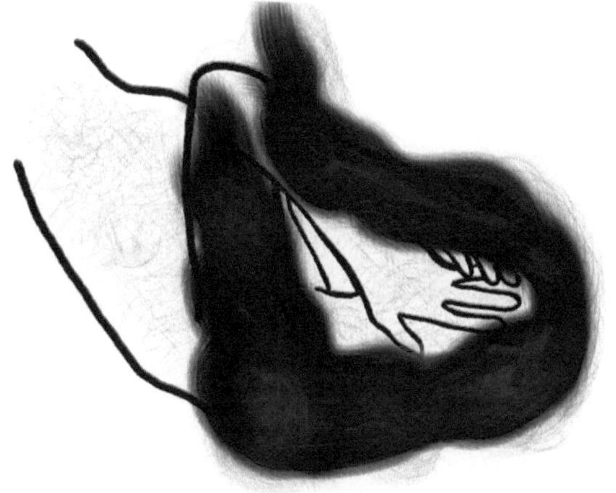

I've felt the gravel lift up from under my feet,
Incapable of functioning,
after endless days of weeping,
unconditional arms sweep me, sworn to protect, when I am in agony.
Blessed am I to have the one who carried, nurtured and supported my every move.
From pitter patter to flying, to falling, to rising. Such beauty, even the clouds part to shine for her.

My confidant, advocate, sister, teacher, best friend and mother.
Mother, I love you with every fibre of my heart and for you deserve the earth. I will give you the universe.

"Life is hard, tend your garden to see its true beauty. We wilt to bloom." °• *The whispers of my mother* •°

Take my hand, my love,
Let me unveil to you what it is to feel love,
Let me introduce you to affection, infatuation, support,
kindness, loyalty, dedication.

When the wants, shifts into a need,
I'll show you the stars,
We can observe from another world

The sun reflects my happiness, the moon is Gods guidance in the darkest times and the stars, well the stars await each ones true love.

Are we so far broken, that all we can do is disagree?...

Maybe the fairy-tale ending, is not meant for you and I.

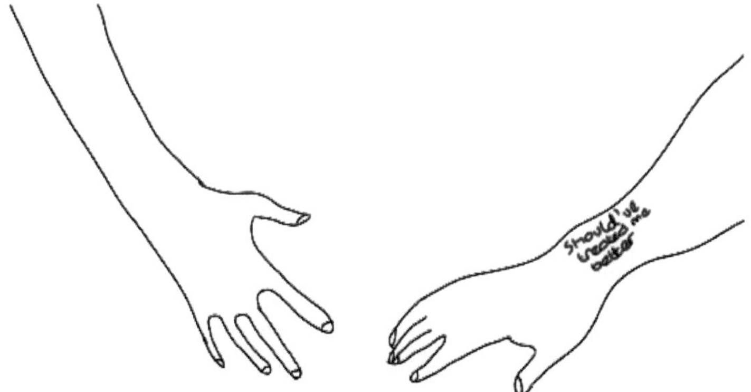

If I am powerfully hard to decipher,

Why do you return to my arms?

Do not attempt to claim that my body is yours.
It is and will always be mine.

Let me remind you, that whilst I may or may not invite you, you are a guest in this temple.

•do not overstep your boundaries, respect me as you would silk or honey.

Can we be happy...?
Together?!
Unconditionally!!
For this life time?!
In every lifetime?
We'll find one another.

Can we?

I am not your doll,
Do not play with my hair to the way you like,
Or encase me in your prism cage...
Do not think that because I am small, you can intimidate me, or, play with what little compassion I have.
I will override every subliminal error you have deterred inside.
I am mighty in the ways you had never hoped.
Your words may seem full but without interaction they could be empty.
Just because you hold my heart,
Do not falter and think that you are irreplaceable!

Your toxicity in which you disguised as devotional
security,
or,
the falsified mentality of which you concocted and
unknowingly revealed to be a premature calamity.
Is what will make you appear as a delusional dream,
later unbeknownst.

•I am free as the unblemished harp strung vibrations wavering... you will find yourself unsuccessful to confine the innocence in me.

Falling.

Little sheds,

As each day passes,

This hole deepens,

Continues to feed,

Continues to starve... Me.

. *A sensual love likeminded is exceptionally unique.*

. *Be as creative as you are with your mouth.*

. *Stretch and entangle as you oscillate under my skin.*

He fills me,

With gratitude,

Kisses the unpleasant flaws

I seek nothing more,

The owner of my heart,

Who produces everything that I crave.

Imperfect yet unsullied to this mind.

At times…

When I am without a sound.

It is not because I do not have anything to say, I have plenty.

It is purely for admiration,

Ocean filled thoughts,

The collective flip book moment,

That is your princely smile,

How our lips feel when they meet.

Tell me, what it is that you feel, when our eyes lock?

I mourn that of which was the reflection of myself. Whilst also blossoming into a stronger flawed version who loves me.

I loved you,
The love shown before you was pain
so I could not love enough
Thus resulting in chaos.

I respect myself yes,
but to feel complete within myself
I was at a loss.
I was not whole.

Remember the feel of my hands as they slipped through yours...

The sweet taste of our lips as they match each groove, as perfectly as a super moon rises in the night skies.

The gaze of our eyes as they catch and admire from afar.
As this is a surrealistic delectation that I explore with the foreseeable marido of my crianças, the amor de minha vida.

- *When you feel her hand brush against your face, your hair, your chest, feel my hand and reminisce on how much I am no longer embraced in your arms or enticed to your enchantment.*

I'll bury my emotions deep with the rest of the suppressed thoughts of you.

How heavy my heart feels without you.

Do my tears appeal appetising to you?

I'm guilty of waiting for you.

* *My whole life, I have waited for you...*

* *Here, lay with me, I will kiss your scars and relinquish your nightmares*
* *Remember my scent that lingers.*

After all this time you are still my muse.
I'm aware that I disappoint myself.
Yet I would rather sit under the sun in acceptance than to be buried in denial.

I should snip the vines and burn the galleria of us imprinted in my mind

However you were <u>a</u> one or at least you should have been <u>the</u> one.

Tell me...
Would you mind if I shredded and scattered your heart in to the air only to drown?

•That is how I feel without your love •

There is nothing left for you merely the shadows of our memories if you walk away.
There is lost love only should you no longer hold on.

•In the wake of your absence... the impact you had on my surrealistic dreams will become non-existent.

I envision us creating art using our minds.

The waters to twist the tides and empower the oceans.

The strong winds to ignite the roaring fire.

The explosion to melt the icebergs no need for a collision...

•

WOW!

•

~ How I imagine us in love

Bordering earth to body enthralled yet flummoxed by the leman I ache for.

Distance and time does not make the heart grow fonder, in fact one becomes artic cold.

Once again perplexed by the eventual fated visions of my significant other alternating.

•*How I feel when I'm in and out of your presence.*

His aura reaches me...

How?!

From such a great distance, this I do not know...

His spirit calls out for me, deprived of refuelling from my energy.

Knock knock

Louder and louder as each day surpasses.

You taught me how to love,

** You also taught my heart how to exist despite being fragmented.*

If I have ever loved you
Know that I projected with my all.
If you have let me down
Know that my heart has self repaired

I do not forget.
Yet I will always cleanse my chambered heart in the oceans under the moon

My spirit is classic,
My compassion elasticated,
Unconfined, uncompelled and liberated.

I am a girl inside a woman, No!

I am a woman,
I am the light in which you reach out to,

I am love,
Despite the cracks through the peaks, of which I feel great pain,
I soar,

I am not a lover,
I am your future.

I no longer am your fool,
To ignore, to patronise, to objectify, to belittle, to lie to, to play judge, jury and executioner to.

Of all my many flaws, being soft hearted and accepting less than I deserve, has to be one of the worst. No longer shall I welcome such unapologetic, ill-mannered, ungracious demeanour

Do not tell me what to think,
How to feel,
What I should or should not say!!!
You do not lecture me
You are not me…

I will not play my part in your soap drama,
I'm forever changed,
I will not kneel at your command,
Do you understand?!
Exactly what I mean??
Do you?
Understand?!

Do not call me pretty,
I am more than a face,
A face in which appearances shadow itself.
You should call me intellectual, strong willed, self-reliant, emulous, demure, spiritual, peaceful yet tigerish the epitome of the sun.
I do not dress in hopes that it appeases you, nor for your approval via whistles, motor horns, or, to grope me.
This is all for the satisfaction of myself.

For the next time you contemplate calling me Barbie, succulent or beautiful, remember we as women are much more than the fanatical fantasy image you conjure.

I am a puma...

I am a dream...

I am the moon, sun and stars combined,

I am a canyon...

I am a Lotus and Sakura conjoined.

I am elegance...

I am water,

I am
Free
To be me

To make another feel guilty for your own mistake, manipulation darling.
To then make others seem as though you're hurting, that is the creation of a master tactician.

•Piece by piece I feel you taking away a part of myself... unravelling the cloak of self-love that I spun like silk to my skin. Yet, when I attempt to rid myself of your venom, the drug kicks in and you tighten the grip.

I was never yours to tame,
For the wolf within
Longs to be acknowledged and loved
bountifully.

I seek
another as
my equal,
not a
master.

I shunned the light,
Hissed at the birds that sung to heal my pain.
I told the winds to guide me to peace.
Yet, they led me to you.

•The deep connection between my flowing spirit to the universe, in which openly became acquainted with a love that will grace my future with complete serenity and our former selves who were linked from the first kiss.

Oh, how you mistakenly perceive me as a deer...
How brazen of you,
To think I could ever be at your beck,
I am a panther.

Funny how I loved being in my own silence. Until I met you.

If I were to die today,
Do not speak of how much you loved me!
Think of how much your words could have meant then...

You always did love the limelight.
Yet you failed to acknowledge the sun before you.

• *I was your Amazonian fighting a path based on the words from the man I loved, I was your ray of light. Your sign of protection to uplift you. I know now, you fed alternative little lies to those close as you did to me.*
Your little white lies created a large black hole.

Do you hear my song as though you are in reverie?

Through the winds?

Pursue the moonlight it will lead you to me like a beacon.

The rain I have used as a siren luring you out.

I have cried an ocean and inspired a volcanic storm

You are the piece of earth that I've been missing.

Sirens Song°•

We thought that our love was indestructible,
That together we were untouchable,
Our spirits bound for eternity even in reincarnation.
We were assassins against those that put the targets on one another.
But like the sun fades behind the beautiful fluffed clouds,
So did our love for one another.

•*Never did it fade it, simply hid like we do behind the trees* ✾

Wrap me in layers of paint
Watch as it hardens, as my care for the state of this vicious place plummets

You think that it is normal
to visualize a woman
beneath her fabrics

Yet you feel disgust when
we speak of our period and
bodies experiences

Clearly you are not worthy
of a natural woman if you
of think this unholy.

Fly, fly away.
All the emotions you spew.
Bubble and toil,
Is all that you knew.

Promises spewed on a daily basis,
Fake apologies and back handed comments,
Shadowed by the clouds of my dreams of you and I,

You may not have shared my pain,
Yet you will definitely feel withdrawal from my absence.

Your timing was always impeccable...
You cannot wait until I am unobtainable, to decide it is the right time to proclaim your intentions.

Unveil the truths that are edging to crawl of that tongue.

Speak up, future one, hide no longer •

I cannot contemplate how...
How must you feel?
To succumb to a love who no longer acknowledges you,
repeatedly.

O what an agony it is to have a mind which deteriorates, slowly yet, my love if I could show you the way my heart flutters when I remember and oh, how I fall in love again with you just as the oceans kisses the sands, we would dance to the rhythm and the birds would sing.

My dreams are getting realer, so my feelings are getting stronger.

° I travelled through the depths of darkness just to feel the light from your touch.

Kiss me underneath a pool full of cherry blossom petals,

°Attend to my soul as you ignite my mind.

I wonder when our spirits are free,
Who it is you will seek.
Will it be me?
You knew no love is as greater as mine for you,
Yet you were curious to explore.
So I wonder...
Will it be the love you've been longing for?
Will it be I that you pursue?

The only thing that kept me flowing was thinking that she was just a phase.

A phase?!
How foolish of me?

To consider forgiveness was an option,
That you were sterilised and would not seep in to her pus infected wounds once again.
A statue formed by medusa herself.

I let you breach the huge tower I had been protected in,
And now I cannot seem to lay my eyes without you by my ear.

I admired you, like I admire the sun when it rises.
But like the sun does not admire me back during a sunset, neither do you.

Since you no longer can appreciate the imperfections I contain, I will cradle the sands to keep me warm.

It sinks, and it caves, deeper than deep.
As it ruptures and disconnects five thousand feet now.
It summons... it drifts.
It calms and it roars.
The sun had come out,
Yet the dark it recalls.
Again, and again,
Piece here and piece there,
Lift up, crash down,
Tut, tut drown out.

I seemed to have lost my voice,
Can you find it?

Have you taken it?

I do not sing,
I do not talk.

I drown in silence these days,
My mind is as dark as the deepest part of the oceans.
I am lost for words,
I was quick witted and dazzling.
Now I am lifeless and cannot seem to rid the anchor of my waist.

...
All since you and I divided.

Do not promise me sweet tomorrows if you no longer wish to wait for what is only mine to give?!

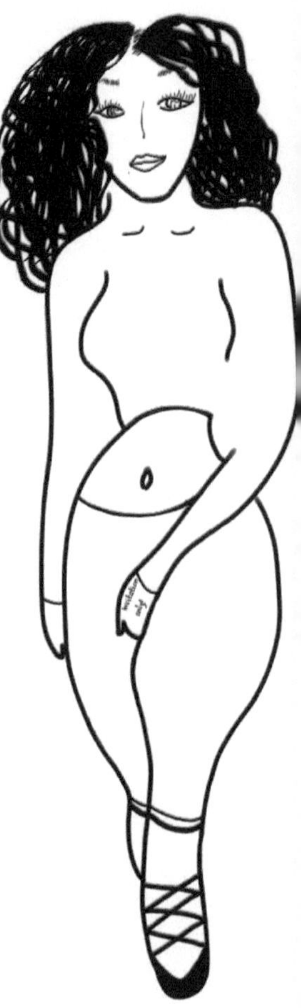

° You cannot pressure my judgement of when you deserve to be united with my soul.

We are underestimated, undermined, undervalued, and condescendingly spoken to

Ladies we are also courageous like the Amazons, we are not submissive, nor are we fools.

We are compassionate, intelligent, and exquisite, we are daughters, sisters, aunts, wives, mothers, mee-maws. Inspirations to each other, we shall not be side-lined, we are prominent, we are sacred, and we are conceivers.

.

.

.

.

We are momentous.

•*Do not blame basic human nature to be cruel or animalistic calamities, or, claim it is merely the persona of a desynchronised heart.*

Here take a stem from my garden and grow it in memory of me. So that you remember that whilst we loved each other once and maybe always will, we can accept that it is now a thing of the past, do not wait for me.

I dreamt that you had come back to me only to tear out my heart

along the floor the following day.

To confess your love and appeal to the soft part of my nature and

profess your deepened apologises.

To chain me with your arms against my ribs

and claim that we will create our version of eden together.

My sweet, darling, love, for you I would recreate any moment, but

most of all the first day we met.

To the one who made the thirteen year old version of myself, feel like I did not matter to the world.

To the one who attempted to make me his prey at fourteen,

To the one who claimed me, when I was never his and rid me of my virtue at seventeen and later on my sanity.

How, dare, you!

For you had all put a hit on the shell of my body and a hex on my mind!

Today I will cleanse away the darkness you have confined me to.

No longer shall I silently sit or cry in sorrow for your sins.

We are reincarnations of our former selves and I have fallen for every version of you.

Oh why had you forsake me, when we needed to be whole.
My blood was scorching whilst I was drowning in my own fluids,
My organs were faltering, my mind advising me to rest now and my heart nagging the body screaming carry on further.

We were strong…
that was until you were stripped, but my goodness it appears that I am starting to recognise you once more, it took some time, I was lost but now I see, you have solved the riddle I laid deep, to find yourself that is.

Sincerely,

Hello me.

Copyright © 2018 SaraFlorença

Instagram: @SaraFlorenca

ISBN 978-1-5272-2937-2

www.ingramcontent.com/pod-product-compliance
Ingram Content Group UK Ltd.
Pitfield, Milton Keynes, MK11 3LW, UK
UKHW041844200726
13854UKWH00005BA/2069

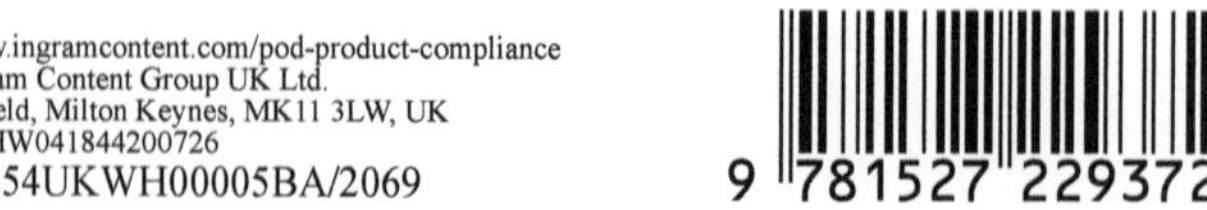

9 781527 229372